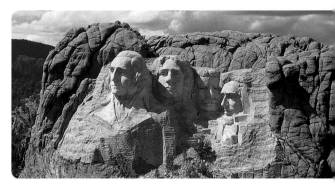

This book is dedicated to all who cherish America's history as a vast heritage of people and events–some heroic, some in glorious, but all part of America's epic struggle to come of age– and to all who know that understanding the past is essential to dealing with the present.

MOUNT RUSHMORE

THE STORY BEHIND THE SCENERY®

by Lincoln Borglum

Lincoln Borglum, content to stay in the shadow of his famous father, Rushmore's sculptor Gutzon Borglum, was the steady influence that kept the day-to-day construction work going on the mountain, enabling the sculptor to devote his time to creative aspects of the carving. Thus Lincoln was more responsible for its successful completion than is commonly realized. Gutzon had taught him his art well, and ever since Lincoln was a toddler, his father had kept him at his side. So it was not surprising that his son emerged as his "right arm" on the project that was to astound the world. Lincoln Borglum was a noted sculptor in his own right and received many commissions before his death on January 27, 1986.

Mount Rushmore National Memorial, located in western South Dakota, set aside in 1925, preserves the sculpted heads of presidents Washington, Jefferson, Lincoln, and Theodore Roosevelt.

Front cover and Page 1: photos by K. C. DenDooven. Inside front cover (early Kodachrome 1935): photo by Lincoln Borglum. Pages 2/3: The four faces, photo by Grant Heilman.

Edited by Mary L. VanCamp. Book design by K. C. DenDooven.

Eighteen Printing, 2009 • New Version

Beauty is like a soul that hovers over the surface of form. Its presence is unmistakable, in art or in life….It is nowhere; it is everywhere; it is in us. The measure of its revelation

depends on the measure of our own soul-consciousness, the boundaries of our own spirit....Beauty is as undefinable as spirit, and yet it is the dominating force in civilization.

Gutzon Borglum

The Mount Rushmore Story

George Washington, Father of the Nation.

It has been called a "shrine" of democracy, and it is! One does not escape the spiritual quality of the experience here at Mount Rushmore. It wakens response in the hearts of the most complacent of citizens, lights the faces of the most cynical of observers, hushes the complaints of tired travelers, young and old, and quickens the step of the world-weary.

Why should this be so? What is it about these faces carved in cold granite that can evoke such feelings of love of country and the sheer joy of being an American, that one no longer cares how in vogue these feelings may or may not be?

Pride? Yes. Pride that here is a true wonder of the world that didn't just happen to be in this land by a whim of nature. Pride that this was an accomplishment born, planned, and created in the minds and by the hands of Americans for Americans. Pride in the

High above the plains, in what is the heartland of America, a colossus rises to greet the expectant eye of the traveler. Nothing imagined can equal the reality of the view one beholds—first framed in the tunnel archways of the Iron Mountain Road, then caught in panoramas from viewpoints across the canyon.

Finally, the overwhelming size of the sculpture draws you hypnotically up the Avenue of Flags to stand on the viewing terrace, as millions have done before, to gaze in silent awe at this statue that, incredibly, was carved from a mountain.

Theodore Roosevelt, Protector of the Working Man.

"This is what it means to be an American"

*T*homas Jefferson, the Expansionist.

*A*braham Lincoln, Preserver of the Union.

four great presidents whose faces reflect the dignity of the heritage that belongs to Americans. Pride in knowing that sons and daughters of generations uncountable will stand here in contemplation, just as we have done. An over-emotional, super-patriotic assessment?

Perhaps. But something so inspiring, so uplifting as this monument must serve a lofty purpose—and it was this purpose for which it was in fact created.

So call it a shrine, monument, memorial—what you will—as you turn away to once again enter the heedless world, there is a fullness of spirit and a lightening of the heart that were not there before. There is an awareness that cannot find expression in words, but no words are needed.

The astounding monument on Mount Rushmore says it all for us—the too busy or too reticent or too sophisticated. There on the mountain the sculptor has spoken eloquently with his art, an eloquence that says simply, "This is what it means to be an American!"

*"**T**here is something here that is related to God in His Heaven that relates ourselves to a universe of gods which super-civilzation, as I see it, seems ever to be reaching towards."*

GUTZON BORGLUMM
NOVEMBER, 1930.

The Incredible Idea

Mount Rushmore has been described as the dream of one man, made a reality by another and, so it was. The nucleus of the idea that was to turn a mountain into a super-colossus of human figures germinated in 1923 in the fertile mind of Doane Robinson. At age 66 he was a venerable and beloved fixture in South Dakota, having founded the state historical society in 1901 and served as state historian ever since.

His idea—"an idea as bold, brilliant, beautiful, and as fragile as a rainbow in the western sky"—was that somewhere in the vicinity of the Needles, in the Black Hills of South Dakota, a monument of gigantic proportions could be carved, perhaps the likenesses of Lewis and Clark, Red Cloud, John C. Fremont, or other great heroes of western history. Such a spectacular attraction, Robinson felt, would serve to bring thousands of tourists to the area and give a much-needed boost to South Dakota's economy.

The idea began to catch in the imagination of a few people, none more ardent or loyal in his support than Peter Norbeck, then a United States Senator from South Dakota and former governor of the state. Others were not so enthusiastic, saying that such a carving would be too expensive, or that it would be a desecration of God's own creation. It was Doane Robinson who wrote my father, Gutzon Borglum, in August 1924, inviting him to come to the Black Hills to see if there was a site suitable for carving such a monument.

LINCOLN BORGLUM

***T**he sculptor and His son Lincoln ride the aerial tramway which ran from base operations to the top of the Roosevelt head, transporting supplies and materials.*

THE CHALLENGE TO CARVE A MOUNTAIN

His proposal could not have found a warmer reception in any other sculptor's heart. Born of Danish parents who had crossed an ocean to pioneer in the West, my father had been taught to love America. Intensely patriotic, he promoted his country enthusiastically and at every opportunity—and he could think in the proportions that the project called for.

At the time Robinson's letter arrived, my

"...an Idea as Bold, Brillant, Beautiful and as Fragile As a Rainbow in the Western sky."

Washington and Lincoln survey the Black Hills country from a lofty 5,675 feet. The ancient granite contains many different minerals brought to the surface by eons of alternating uplift and depression.

RIKKI THOMPSON

father was already a sculptor of note, having attained a popularity and a reputation on both sides of the Atlantic. At this moment he was involved in a project of similar proportions, a monument to honor the heroes of the Civil War, to be carved in bas relief on Stone Mountain, Georgia.

This monument was never to reach completion under his hands, but it perhaps served a purpose, as far as the South Dakota project was concerned, in establishing Gutzon Borglum as a man who was not afraid of the challenge of carving a mountain.

So in September 1924, we came to the Black Hills—my father, Major Jesse Tucker (who was his right-hand assistant at Stone Mountain), and me. I was only twelve at the time, but was accustomed to being included in everything my father did; he felt there was no better teacher than practical experience. Accompanied by our guides and several prominent South Dakotans, we set out on September 24th to explore the area where Robinson hoped my father would find a site for the proposed monument.

Borglum on "Bigness"

Colossal art has [a] value—human and soul-stirring—that should be incorporated permanently in all National expression—consciously and deliberately in scale with its importance [and] with the people whose li[ves] it expresses.

Some few years ago, a sculptor visited me who showed me the head of a pin, on which he had carved the head of a president. Quite apart from my feelings regarding the purpose, the meaninglessness of this...product of the magnifying glass and patience, I began to think more seriously on the subject of making things larger and better. This pin-head sculptor was shaping the dimensions of his life and soul...into smaller and more cramped dimensions. In thinking of this, I realized how the whole process of life in its healthy form [is expansive] in character; nature [grows] from within out; understanding enlarges one's visions, one's happiness, multiplies the forms of pleasure; includes always—by selection excludes but never diminishes. And with this thought, I called to mind the value of natural phenomena to the imagination and the use of the extraordinary in all the classic fairy tales...I recalled distinctly that volume, great mass, has a greater emotional effect upon the observer than quality of form; that quality of form (when it is understood) affects the mind; volume shocks the nerve or soul-centers and is emotional in its effect.

...I recall thinking of the adventures of Thor, of Hercules, of storms at sea. Dante's Vita Nuova, Milton's Paradise Lost, with all their splendor, art and beauty, have never affected me like [those adventures or] the thunder when it cracks and rolls over Rushmore and fairly pours around Washington's head like a Niagara of sound. You can fairly feel the wave lengths as they strike the neighboring walls....

There is something here that is related to God in His Heaven aeons older than the pin-head sculptor, something that relates itself and ourselves to a universe of gods which super-civilization, as I see it, seems ever to be reaching towards.

—From The Black Hills Engineer, November, 1930.

I remember vividly the long horseback ride through the spectacular granite "Needles." By the next evening we had ridden or walked over many, many miles of its rough terrain. But the tall, irregular rock of the Needles was badly weathered, and my father felt the proportions were wrong for carving. He was still very interested in the project, however, and that evening, back in Rapid City, wrote a statement energetic in its enthusiasm.

This was truly a mountainous area and, at the time of this visit, only a sparsely populated mining district with few roads. But the scenery was magnificent, and South Dakota's hope to develop and advertise it as a tourist attraction seemed well founded. Rich granite pegmatites, deep canyons, and sparkling caves abounded here. Clear streams teemed with trout. Bright flowers, cheerful songbirds, and sleek wildlife filled the ponderosa-pine forests.

Within all this were the impressive rock formations of the Harney Range that my father described in his statement to the press before we left as a "veritable garden of the gods." Here he could carve a memorial so high up that its inaccessibility would protect it from the vandalism he feared—a memorial that would be located deep in the center, the core, of the nation.

A Mountain is Chosen

So the next August we returned. Setting out again with our guides and a group of eager South Dakotans, we had covered almost every rocky upthrust of the Harney Range when we came to the massive, gray peak known as Mount Rushmore. This was the monolith my father had been searching for—a gigantic mountain of solid granite, towering above the surrounding peaks and well separated from them. Most important, the major face of the rock was to the southeast, an aspect essential for maximum sunlight during the daytime hours. As he talked in that positive, mesmerizing way of his, I began to see in the great peak the colossal mountain sculpture he could create here.

Sylan Lake, in Custer State Park, was visited by the Borglums in their search for a peak that could be carved into a lasting memorial. The lake's proximity to Harney Peak, its abundant trout and scenic beauty make this a favorite vacationing ground for South Dakotans and tourists alike.

RUSS FINLEY

JEFF GNASS

The rugged "Needles" area of the Black Hills was the first site proposed for the carving; however, Borglum found that the granite here was too weathered and unstable.

"But Here we have such stone large enough for not one but three or Four or five figures."

A page from the sculptor's journal reveals in his typical scrawl his thoughts at the end of a two-day hike in search of a site for the monument. The figures in the sketch were drawn by Borglum "in the round," as they were first envisioned when the Needles was still under consideration as a site. The journal entry (punctuation edited) reads:

He had become convinced, however, that the proposed theme—heroes of western history—was too regionally circumscribed, too insignificant nationally, for what they had in mind. Doane Robinson agreed, and soon my father was drawing sketches of Washington, of Lincoln and Washington, and then of Jefferson, Lincoln, and Washington—in the round, as the carving was first envisioned—and mulling the entire concept over in his mind.

This was a project which fired his imagination tremendously, a thing that had never been done. A monument for the great nation he loved, on the scale of these mountains that dominated the prairies, located in the heartland of the nation. The peak that he had selected stood in the center of the Harney Range, the pinnacle of the entire area, in the sacred land of the Lakota Nation and a part of the Louisiana Purchase, the first great expansion of the United States.

He had found his mountain and would accept the commission. Moreover, he would offer a concept of the undertaking far nobler than even that which had been proposed. My father was later to write of his thoughts at this time:

A monument's dimensions should be determined by the importance to civilization of the events commemorated. We are not here trying to carve an epic, portray a moonlight scene, or write a sonnet; neither are we dealing with mystery or tragedy, but rather the constructive and the dramatic moments or crises in our amazing history. We are coolheadedly, clear-mindedly setting down a few crucial, epochal facts regarding the accomplishments of the Old World radicals who shook the shackles of oppression from their light feet and fled despotism to people a continent; who built an empire and rewrote the philosophy of freedom and compelled the world to accept its wiser, happier forms of government.

We believe the dimensions of national heartbeats are greater than village impulses, greater than city demands, greater than state dreams or ambitions. Therefore, we believe a nation's memorial should, like Washington, Jefferson, Lincoln, and Roosevelt, have a serenity, a nobility, a power that reflects the gods who inspired them and suggests the gods they have become.

Friday, Aug. 14, 1925

Friday, Aug. 13-14, 1925

Left game lodge at 7 a.m. in car with Lincoln and Colonel Shade. Met horses 12 miles on road and then entered trail to interior of park back of Harney. Party: Shoemaker, Shade, Sanders, Mr. Bryan. And proceeded in northwest direction towards Mt. Rushmore. Camped at 12 at foot of mountain, about 18 yards from base, and after lunch scaled the mountain. Found stone satisfactory and schists, weather marks, and natural seams.

I had been doubtful of finding stone which would admit of detail or would have masses large enough to develop a continuous form like the chest, shoulders, and torso of a figure two hundred feet high. But here we have such stone large enough for not one but three or four or five figures. A group of the Empire Makers: Jefferson, Lincoln, Roosevelt.

The trip was wonderful, full every moment of the most dramatic of mountain scenery and hazard[ous] to horse and rider. The shoulder of Rushmore is far and away the best that I have seen.

Colonel Shade took Lincoln and myself to Sylvan Lake and gave us horses to climb the Harney Peak. We took lunch and did this. The view disclosed three great cliffs: Rushmore, Baldy, and Sugar Loaf. Rushmore still remains the choice. We returned to lodge at 5 p.m. and dined, bathed, and retired. Tomorrow we go to Deadwood.

*They helped shape events which had
such a dramatic impact upon the country
and were spread out over the 18th, 19th and 20th centuries—
the life of the nation so far.*

Plans, Problems and Politics

CHARLES D' EMERY

Gutzon Borglum plants a 48-star flag at the summit of Mount Rushmore for the 1925 dedication of the mountain.

The part of South Dakota in which the Black Hills lies was, in 1924, a very isolated area. The closest town was Keystone, near the confluence of Battle and Grizzly creeks. Here, during the 1880s, the Holy Terror mine had produced large quantities of gold, until the water ran into it faster than pumps in those days could handle it. The roads were rough to nonexistent, often impassable, but they were used by only a few people, for at the time the carving was begun Keystone was pretty much a deserted village, with very little active mining being done in the area.

Mount Rushmore was itself completely inaccessible except on foot or by horseback or horse-drawn wagons, and the only approach to the mountain was by old logging roads, long since abandoned.

MOUNTAIN NAMED IN 1885

Few people knew the name of this wilderness peak 5,725 feet above sea level. In fact, until 1885 it didn't even have a name. That year a New York attorney, Charles E. Rushmore, hired to do some title investigation in the Black Hills, was looking over

President Coolidge (in ten-gallon hat) speaks at the 1927 ceremony launching the construction work.
Flanking him are Senator Norbeck and Governor Bulow of South Dakota. Senators Fess (Ohio) and McMaster (South Dakota) are at far right. (Early hand-tinted glass plate.)

the country on horseback and, curious about the tall peak, asked his prospector-guide about it. The rough miner, given a chance to gently rib his eastern companion, replied (so the story goes), "Hell, it never had a name, but from now on we'll call the damn thing Rushmore."

The name stuck, but until the day it was selected as the site for the huge memorial my father was to carve, there weren't many who cared what the mountain was called, and it wasn't until 1930, when the work on the mountain was already in progress, that the name was officially recognized. (Charles Rushmore was later to become one of the earliest contributors to the memorial, with a gift of $5,000.)

This was the mountain, then, that was to bring throngs to South Dakota. Senator Norbeck was frank in his disappointment of the choice. This particular peak, he said, was too remote, too hard to reach. Robinson, on the other hand, was ecstatic.

If Borglum could find a way to carve this mountain, Robinson knew he could find a way to bring people to it.

His optimism seemed to be vindicated when, on October 1, 1925, 3,000 people struggled over the rough trails to Mount Rushmore to attend its dedication as a memorial. Dad loved pageantry and ceremony, and this—the first of six colorful dedications for the monument—set the precedent. A band played, and there were cavalry salutes and speeches by Norbeck, Robinson, my father, and others. A group of Rapid City women had made six huge (18' by 24') flags depicting the periods when other nations ruled over the territory now the United States. These were hoisted in rapid succession in a flag-raising ceremony Dad had planned. My father was no fool—he knew the value of the publicity that attended such goings on and the contributions it might generate.

The warmth of sunrise suggests the warmth of the real-life Lincoln as he gazes with compassion on the great nation he preserved and inspired.

MANY DIFFICULT PROBLEMS

His decision made and announced to the world, my father was faced with many immediate and difficult problems. The basic problem was always money, the lack of which plagued the project throughout its duration. He was in much demand for his work, with many interesting commissions coming in at the time to his studios in Stamford, Connecticut, and San Antonio, Texas, and it looked as though these funds would be needed.

South Dakota's governor was reluctant to endorse the project and so, in spite of the efforts of Robinson and other hard-working supporters, financial backing in the state legislature did not seem to be forthcoming.

Dad never intended that the project at Rushmore would dominate the rest of his life. His original plan, one that had been accepted by Doane

***W*ashington gazes benignly over the vast nation** *that America has become since he "fathered" it in 1776. Situated in the most prominent position of the four, Washington seems as large as the mountain itself.*

Robinson's group, the state-appointed Mount Harney Memorial Association, was that he would create the models, and supervise the progress and accuracy of the carving, leaving him time to devote to his other commissions.

The actual mechanical part of the work—the routine tasks of engineering, the day-to-day, hardrock labor—were to be in the charge of Major Jesse Tucker, the only other man in the world with any practical knowledge of mountain-carving and its problems. He was familiar with the stone-removal techniques developed at Stone Mountain, and he had worked with my father and the Du Pont Company of Delaware when the new and exacting techniques of carving stone with dynamite first evolved.

With Tucker superintending the work, my father expected to be free of managerial responsibilities. But things didn't turn out as planned.

***T**he selection of Theodore Roosevelt as the fourth president for the memorial met with controversy. Some felt he was too recent to be so honored, but President Coolidge added the decisive reason for "Teddy's" inclusion—that he had been the first president who had actively protected the rights of the working man.*

Major Tucker became unhappy with financial arrangements and returned to his home in Florida in 1929, so that early in the project my father curtailed his other work to give the mountain carving his undivided attention.

He was, of course, to plan the design and then work out the engineering problems and techniques. There were no guidelines or precedents on mountain carving, beyond those he himself had established at Stone Mountain, and no skilled carvers available. He must train local miners to be assistant sculptors. These challenges may have overwhelmed a lesser man, but my father was, after all, an artist—a man with a special destiny and a larger vision.

Jefferson, who always yearned to see the West, can now survey to his heart's content the country that he sent Captains Lewis and Clark to explore in 1804.

Still not clearly defined was the matter of what was to go on the mountain, which geologists estimated would surely last a hundred thousand years, perhaps a half million. What theme would justify taking a mountain and carving it into something worthy of that mountain?

My father, an immigrant's son who had himself studied and worked abroad, wanted the mountain to represent American ideals. He felt that a memorial of this magnitude should have meaning for all citizens of the country, that it should be dedicated to American culture and civilization— to democracy. This lofty mountain deserved to tell the story of the entire nation, not just part of it. The sculptor's challenge here was more than carving images from stone.

With these ideals in mind, he continued to develop the plan for Rushmore already started with his sketches on our return trip to South Dakota. The

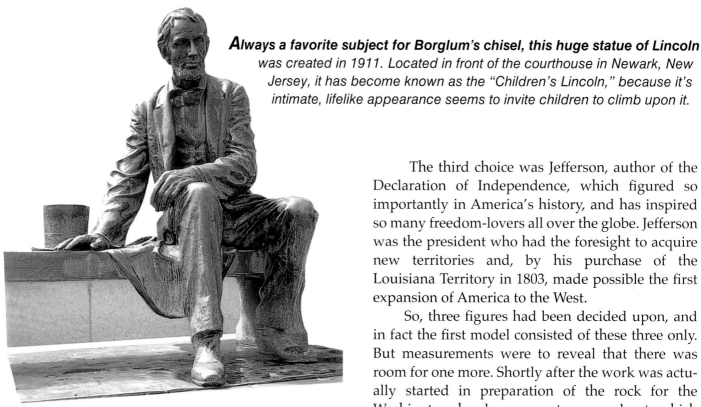

Always a favorite subject for Borglum's chisel, this huge statue of Lincoln was created in 1911. Located in front of the courthouse in Newark, New Jersey, it has become known as the "Children's Lincoln," because it's intimate, lifelike appearance seems to invite children to climb upon it.

LINCOLN BORGLUM COLLECTION

final concept was a memorial—not to individuals, but to the founding, preservation, growth, and development of the nation, as embodied in four presidents who had never lost sight of the simple concept on which it was founded: "Man has a right to be free and to be happy."

SELECTING THE PRESIDENTS

Washington had been the uncontested first choice, as the father of the infant democracy and a man whose strength and dignity were a source of inspiration for the nation in its new independence. The choice of Lincoln was also without controversy. My father felt it absolutely essential to include Lincoln, the man who had held the country together during its greatest trial and who was, he felt, one who truly understood the tenets of democracy.

A life-long admirer of Lincoln, my father had read everything he could find about Lincoln. He had carved a marble bust of Lincoln for the rotunda of the Capitol in Washington, D.C., which Robert Lincoln described, in 1908, as "the most extraordinarily good portrait of my father I have ever seen." The huge statue of a seated Lincoln he created in 1911 was his own favorite work, and a very popular one.

Many observers have remarked that the compassionate face of Lincoln is the most skillfully carved of the four faces on Mount Rushmore. If this is true, it is no doubt because of my father's great reverence and love for Lincoln, his favorite subject.

The third choice was Jefferson, author of the Declaration of Independence, which figured so importantly in America's history, and has inspired so many freedom-lovers all over the globe. Jefferson was the president who had the foresight to acquire new territories and, by his purchase of the Louisiana Territory in 1803, made possible the first expansion of America to the West.

So, three figures had been decided upon, and in fact the first model consisted of these three only. But measurements were to reveal that there was room for one more. Shortly after the work was actually started in preparation of the rock for the Washington head, an event came about which helped to finalize the fourth and most controversial choice: In 1927 Coolidge came to South Dakota.

President Coolidge's highly publicized choice of South Dakota's State Game Lodge in Custer State Park as the Summer White House (from where he made his famous "I do not choose to run" speech) is important in the story of Rushmore. The president became very inter-ested in the carving and entered the project enthusiastically. (The press had a field day with the story of how my father obtained the president's attention by dropping a large wreath of flowers from an airplane onto the front lawn of the Summer White House.)

The subject of whether Theodore Roosevelt would become the fourth face had already been tossed around verbally and in the press. Some said he was too recent to be venerated in such a lasting way—that the test of his presidency had not been tried by time. But Senator Norbeck was enthusiastic and my father, too, had been inclined toward the choice, having been a personal friend and admirer of the late "Rough Rider."

He had himself argued that it was Roosevelt who saw in the opening of the Panama Canal the realization of the dream of Columbus, and recognized that its completion would greatly hasten the industrial development of the nation by providing quicker access to the West. But it was Coolidge who added the decisive reason for the inclusion of the face of Theodore Roosevelt upon the mountain (a subject on which he was most adamant). I heard him say that Roosevelt was the first president who had actively worked to protect the rights of the working man.

Thus were the four presidents, leaders during four important formative periods of American history, chosen to be immortalized in stone on the mountain in South Dakota. Washington, the founder; Jefferson, the expansionist; Lincoln, the preserver of the Union; and Roosevelt, the protector of the working man and contributor to the industrial growth of the nation.

The events they helped shape, events which had such a dramatic impact upon the country, were spread out over the 18th, 19th, and 20th centuries—the life of the nation so far.

The First Drilling

The first drilling on the mountain was celebrated on August 10, 1927, in a picturesque ceremony. The honored guest speaker was President Coolidge, who arrived clad unfamiliarly in western regalia (including a ten-gallon hat), and astride a horse. My father was lowered in a harness to ceremonially launch the work by drilling the first "points" for the face of Washington (work did not actually commence in earnest until about two months later), followed by more flag-raising ceremonies and speeches.

Coolidge realized fully the difficulties of financing such an enormous project on a local level, and before returning to Washington he suggested to my father that he visit him at the Capitol to discuss the needs for the carving. Perhaps government funds would be available for help in the project. (Coolidge's assessment of the situation did indeed eventually prove correct, and there is no doubt that the president's role in the development of the monument was vital.) It was Coolidge himself who suggested that his dedication speech be printed and distributed in an effort to get money for the monument.

The nationwide publicity attending this public endorsement by the president of the United States for the carving of Mount Rushmore was the impetus the project needed to get underway. Once the carving actually began, the arguments that had been raging in the press among the people of the Black Hills suddenly ceased.

Contributions began to come in from school children, service clubs, small businessmen, and other individuals. Some of the larger contributors at this time were the Dakota Farmer, the Homestake Mine, the Chicago and Northwestern, Burlington, and Milwaukee railroads, Mr. Rushmore, and Senator Coleman Du Pont.

Perhaps the most immediate and practical help was the provision by Mr. Samuel Insull (Northwestern Public Service Company of Huron) of a large diesel generator and two compressors, equipment valued at nearly $20,000. (The compressors lasted throughout the duration of the carving, although we did add to their capacities later.) Soon there was $54,000 with which to begin work; the future looked deceptively rosy.

My father had hoped that private grants, together with help from South Dakota and the Mount Harney Association, could be obtained to finance the project completely. Through the efforts of Doane Robinson, the association had been authorized by the state legislature in 1925 to take on the project. This bill provided no funding, however, and the association remained virtually a dead organization until 1927, when the new governor, W. J. Bulow, became its chairman.

The work was only beginning, and already the money that had been raised in the first flush of publicity was gone. On December 7, 1927, operations closed down for the onset of winter, and no carving at all was done the following year. During this time there was only lukewarm support, and private contributors were few. Many promised, but never delivered, large sums.

Senator Peter Norbeck,
a principal mover in the legislation that funded Rushmore, poses for the sculptor in his studio.

Federal Funding Needed

So, as Coolidge had foreseen, promoters for the mountain were obliged to turn to Washington for federal funds to speed up the work. The South Dakota delegation in Washington, led by the tireless Senator Norbeck and Congressman William

"Temper, **yes**, but **he** never held **a** grudge **each day** **was a brand**-new **day** to **my** father"

Williamson, introduced legislation to provide for federal funding, but technicalities held up passage until February 1929, when Public Law 805 was finally approved.

This law created the Mount Rushmore Memorial Commission, superseding the old Mount Harney Memorial Association. It consisted of 12 presidential appointees—moneyed and influential citizens from all over the nation—whose function it would be to carry out all of the details pertaining to the construction of the memorial. Five of these members were to form the executive committee, of which John Boland, an astute Rapid City business man, was elected chairman. He was to bear most of the financial burden for the memorial's affairs until he resigned in 1938.

The bill provided $250,000 for the purpose of matching, dollar for dollar, any funds obtained from private sources. It was retroactive, thereby matching some funds already donated, so the carving during that summer went full speed ahead, with our great expectations of obtaining more money. We were jubilant; the new law seemed like the answer to all our troubles. But this was 1929, the year of the stock-market crash, and with it the private sources we had counted on dried up completely.

So began a series of innumerable trips to Washington and throughout the country for my father. He didn't welcome the job of fund-raiser, but he was determined to see the completion of the project, and no one could plead more eloquently for the memorial than he, for his enthusiasm was contagious and his positive manner inspired confidence.

Usually the trips to Washington would result in a small appropriation, perhaps enough to keep the work going for a few months, but there were many long periods when there was no money to pay the workers, and no work was accomplished at all. The whole problem of financing resulted in a sort of "start-stop" operation, greatly lengthening the duration of the project. It was not until 1934 that amended legislation provided for funding by direct appropriation, not matching, and from then on, until we shut down in November of 1941, all funds for the monument came from direct appropriation by Congress. Once the government assumed the entire financial burden, the work was halted only when weather demanded.

MOUNT RUSHMORE MEMORIAL COMMISSION

The Mount Rushmore Memorial Commission at first had many responsibilities, including planning for financing, but after 1933 it functioned under the National Park Service, Department of the Interior. In 1938 it was transferred to the Treasury Department, but was returned a year later to the National Park Service. This all came about through various reorganization bills during President Franklin D. Roosevelt's administration.

Much has been written of my father's conflicts with John Boland, chairman of the executive committee of the commission, and others whose job it was to look after the details of administering the project—that his "temperament" and "explosive personality" were the cause of the conflicts.

The truth is that my father had a high regard for Boland and the other administrators, but he could not resign himself to being under the jurisdiction of any branch of government (and the commission was a government body, albeit more independent than most). Control by any regulative or administrative body to him meant rules, directives, paperwork—all the things for which he admittedly had little patience.

As the artist, my father had conceived and planned the work. He wanted to get on with it—to

Gutzon Borglum poses with his wife Mary and son Lincoln for this 1928 photo taken in front of his first studio at Rushmore.

I think it was also true that few shared his vision of the work. Many, many people worked for the memorial in various ways, and the unflagging dedication of Robinson, Norbeck, Williamson, Representative Francis Case, and those close to the project showed their complete faith in my father's ability. But others, sometimes even close friends, failed to comprehend the meaning and importance of the work he was doing.

His greatest support during such times came unfailingly from my mother, Mary Montgomery Borglum. A scholar of languages who had attended Wellesley and received her Ph.D. from the University of Berlin (the first woman to attain such an honor), she had been successfully launched in a career in a New York publishing business when she met and decided to devote her life to Borglum, a man of genius. She understood completely the compelling forces that drove him, of which she later wrote:

> *He [the artist] is inspired* by the same forces that influence the nation's destiny — the greater the period, the greater the art. The artist cannot escape his destiny. Like the "Hound of Heaven" it "pursues him down the years," forces him to leave his home, to go into exile, to combat mountains even, to accomplish what he must.
>
> How else can we explain why a man should abandon a comfortable way of life, among pleasant surroundings, to hurl himself against a gigantic rock, to cling like a human fly to a perpendicular peak, to struggle with hostile human nature, in order to carve against the sky a record which will live on and be an inspiration to future generations, a shrine to be visited, even after the thing it commemorated may have passed.

create, to transform the bare mountainside into the work of art he alone could fully envision. To him the idea was everything; budgeting and other factors were minor details to get out of the way as quickly as possible. But Boland and later the Park Service officials (at first reluctant to have the memorial in their department) were dedicated men who took their work seriously, too. It was the natural conflict between artist and businessman.

So it was, I think, understandable that clashes should occur—the administrators perhaps feeling that my father was indeed temperamental and heedless of the inevitable practicalities involved, and my father feeling that he was being dictated to by people he thought didn't fully grasp the concept and significance of the work.

Those who knew intimately of my father's extreme generosity and gentleness just laughed at charges of his "ungovernable" temper. Temper, yes, but he never held a grudge, and people he had vowed on one day never to speak to again were astonished to be greeted on the following day with a warm smile and a hearty handshake. Each day was a brand-new day to my father.

We had indeed left a "comfortable way of life" at Borgland, my parents' estate in Connecticut, where we had lived many happy years. Here my father had created many of his masterpieces, including his famous "Wars of America" monument now standing in Newark, New Jersey, the Trail Driver's Monument in Texas, and others. He finished all these magnificent pieces of sculpture after first becoming involved with Rushmore. But he was now irrevocably committed to the carving of a mountain in a primitive area of South Dakota, and he often said that only God could keep him from completing his work there.

The first step in the pointing was to locate the point of the nose

Art, Engineering and Dynamite

For guidance in the design of the models, my father had studied photographs, portraits, life masks, and descriptions of the presidents, and then had made his own original interpretations, using the sculptor's tools of light and shadow to create countenances which would indeed have "human character and vitality."

The first design had been completed in the studio in San Antonio, and I was charged with the responsibility of bringing the model to South Dakota during my summer vacation from high school. Falling asleep at the wheel, I went off the road and overturned the car. Fortunately, the presidents' faces (Washington, Jefferson, and Lincoln in this early model) and I were undamaged; only the "mountain" and the car were in need of repair. Dad said of the incident only that it was "easier to repair a broken mountain than a broken boy."

My father, realizing that we would be spending considerable time in South Dakota, bought a ranch about twenty miles southeast of Mount Rushmore, near Hermosa, as a place for us to live. He remodeled the ranch house, made a guest house of the chicken house, and converted the barn into a studio. We made our home on this ranch during the times work on Rushmore was in progress, and when work was shut down, spent the winters in San Antonio.

LINCOLN BORGLUM (Early Kodachrome, 1935)

Gutzon Borglum was a creative person who could see *the future: Granite Rocks into presidental faces. Lincoln Borglum, his son, became the man on the faces, turning granite into the faces we see today.*

Publishers note: Kodachrome was released in 1936. "Early Kodachrome, 1935" refers to experimental film given to Lincoln Borglum for testing by Eastman Kodak. —KCDD

These models were scaled an inch to the foot (every inch on the models represented a foot on the mountain). The figures were to the scale of men 465 feet tall, so that measurements on the completed face of Washington, for instance, would be: face, 60 feet long; nose, 20 feet long; eyes, 11 feet wide; eye projections, 22 inches. Roosevelt's mustache would be 20 feet long, and Lincoln's mole 16 inches across.

The whole sculpture when finished was 185 feet across from the left of Washington's head to the right of Lincoln's head, and 160 feet from the top of the heads to the lowest point on the coats. Can the four figures on Rushmore be considered perfect? A reporter once seriously asked this question of my father and he replied, perhaps not so seriously, that the nose of Washington was an inch too long—but that it would erode enough "to make it exactly right in 10,000 years."

A workman in hanging cage finishing details on Lincoln's left eye. Chains looped across the eye and attached to the pupil are fastened to the cage as a safety precaution. Borglum set high standards for his men. "If they do not follow, they have got to have better ways or good reasons or they take a holiday." (Early Kodachrome, 1936.)

The first scale of Washington was made in a log cabin, the Keystone slaughterhouse, which my father had been using as a temporary studio. (I later purchased this cabin and moved it to its present site at the ranch.) It had become increasingly difficult to work in the midst of the large crowds that were always moving through the building, so a new studio, also log, was constructed at the base of the mountain. A huge window in this studio framed the view of the mountain across the canyon, a view which was soon to be forever transformed.

When the new studio was finished, the Washington model was moved there, and the rest of the design was blocked out in plaster of paris. The models were only an approximation of what was to go on the mountain, intentionally left rough. My father believed that "when a man has finished a `perfect model' he has expressed himself and is through. Finished models should not be made— in them all the creative impulse has expressed itself; the enlargement is inevitably a stillborn, dead, soulless thing."

Preceeding Pages:
The eyes in stone come alive with the early morning sunlight. Photo by Ed Cooper

THE "POINTING MACHINE"

My father had early worked out a system so that untrained miners and laborers could learn to do the work of assistant sculptors, a sort of complicated "sculpt-by-numbers" process that we called pointing, accomplished with the aid of what my father called his "pointing machine."

At the top and center point of the mass which was to be each head, an upright cylindrical shaft was placed, mounted on a base of steel bolted to the mountain—a plate about four feet across its flat surface, upon which was cut the 360 degrees of a circle (sometimes only half a circle). The shaft was held in place by guy cables stiffened with buckles. To this upright shaft a steel beam about 30 feet long was horizontally attached, in a manner much like the spoke in a wheel. This was a movable boom that could be rotated and set on any degree, and was itself divided into measurements.

From the boom hung two mercury-filled plumb-bobs about two feet apart, and above them a six-foot carpenter's level was mounted horizontally on the boom, since it was very important that it be exactly level at all times. Each of the plumb-bobs was immersed in a bucket of oil to hold it steady, and all was suspended on steel piano wire as fine as possible so as to have the least possible wind

*T*he sculptor in his studio within full view of the mountain he was to transform. The model is an early version that contains, for the sculptor's comparison, Jefferson heads in two locations. (This early photograph was reproduced from a hand-tinted glass plate, one of many in this book taken by Charles d'Emery, of Stamford, Connecticut, before color film came into popular use. Borglum admired the work of the enthusiastic d'Emery and often called on him to take photographs of the construction and events at Mount Rushmore for use in fund-raising campaigns.)

resistance. (Critical measurements were done early in the morning, before the wind began to blow.) This wire also was marked with measurements; it could be cranked out to any desired length by means of a device, similar to a fishing reel, mounted on the boom.

A similar steel plate and boom were installed in the same relative position on each model head in the studio below. Measurements were made on the model and enlarged 12 times as they were transferred to the surface of the mountain. Thus a plumb-bob might be set out 10 inches on the boom of the model and 10 feet on its counterpart on the mountain, so that, if the tip of the bob on the small boom was lowered 30 inches and touched a point on the nose, the tip of the corresponding bob on the large boom would come down 30 feet (when the intervening rock had been removed) to touch a corresponding point on the sculpture. The finding of a hidden point, say under the nose, was done by a system of references from the known and marked points.

Accurate measurements could now be taken, rough "points" (as they were called on the work) determined, and an approximation made of the mass necessary for the carving of each head. When the excess stone was removed, a great egg-shaped mass (from three to six feet larger than the final head) would be the result. At this stage, work was halted so my father could observe over a long period of time the effects of light and shadow—the probable

sunlight the head would receive—and thus determine the angle at which it should actually face.

Such experiments resulted in the turning of the head of Washington about twenty degrees further to the south than originally intended, permitting the sun to fall on the north side of his face as late as 1:00 p.m. My father would have preferred to have turned it even further, but the stone left in place for the hair on Washington's left side would not permit further turning.

With the establishment of the center line of the face, down over the forehead beginning at the point of the wig and down midway between the eyebrows, down over the forehead beginning at the point of the wig and down midway between the eyebrows, down over the center of nose, mouth, and chin, we were ready to map the stone for accurate drilling and careful blasting.

The first step in the pointing was to locate the point of the nose, it being the extreme projection on the face. When, using our system of transferring measurements from model to mountain, we had located the approximate end of the nose, we might find perhaps six feet or so too much stone. We made a red dot, drew a circle around the dot and painted on the side of the circle "No. 1, 6'."

The next points to be taken were the ones on each of the frontal bones, for which the great boom had to be swung to the right and left. Here the absolute necessity for great precision in the mechanism

by which we obtained our measurements can be appreciated. Any slight twist or bend in the boom, if not detected and corrected, would result in a distortion in the face itself. We were extremely vigilant to see that such an error did not occur.

INTEGRATION OF ART AND ENGINEERING

The "pointer" was the most important man on the mountain, next to the sculptor, since he was responsible for all measurements and approved all drilling and blasting. In the day-to-day operation, he had to constantly lay out new work so there would be no delay in placing the workmen to the greatest advantage, and he was the one who must be able at all times to tell the sculptor how much stone there was at any given point.

At first the measurements were quite far apart—about one foot—since the stone at that stage

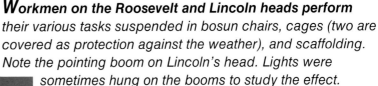

Workmen on the Roosevelt and Lincoln heads perform *their various tasks suspended in bosun chairs, cages (two are covered as protection against the weather), and scaffolding. Note the pointing boom on Lincoln's head. Lights were sometimes hung on the booms to study the effect.*

cally and horizontally, a series of painted marks indicating how much stone to remove at each point. He would set the series of points by drilling each to the required depth, and the surrounding stone would then be taken off to this depth.

As the holes were placed closer together and more care was required, it became more practical to make the depth indications with paint and remake them each time as the stone upon which they were painted was removed. Many of the men became very capable in the art of stonecutting, and could carry on the cutting in a highly skilled manner.

The work was done with a margin of about three inches; this was the stone left for the actual finishing of the features and correcting of the perspective, again requiring my father's closest attention. The entire process was truly an integration of art and engineering, both of equal importance.

The First Face Unveiled

The mountain had been dedicated on October 1, 1925, and drilling commenced on October 4, 1927. On Independence Day 1930, the first face, a recognizable portrait of the first president of the United States, was to be unveiled.

It was now possible to reach Mount Rushmore by automobile, and that day a crowd of 2,500 people gathered to see the face of Washington revealed as the 67' by 39' flag was pulled away, and to hear the sculptor speak of the work on the mountain and his intentions for bringing "human character and vitality" to the "great mass." For the Washington face at that time was not the complete, refined head it is today; then it was merely a rough likeness. He expected the work to go much faster from now on, but had to reckon with the fact that the project had been started during prosperity, and now there was deep depression.

Still, that first triumphant unveiling had a psychological effect, and there was renewed enthusiasm for the memorial and increased determination to see it completed. (The phrase, "shrine of democracy," came into being at this dedication, somewhat altered from a speech by Joseph S. Cullinan, a past chairman of the commission.)

was just being blocked out. But as we progressed toward the final surface the measurements were made much closer together, until finally they were close enough—two or three inches—and the distance between each point a straight line, not curved. Usually these contour points were made at five-degree intervals.

The result was that the driller, facing a section of the mountain, would see before him, both verti-

LINCOLN BORGLUM

LINCOLN BORGLUM

ED COOPER

Tourists continued to find their way to South Dakota, driving over the twisting roads to witness the spectacle of men carving rock with dynamite. The nation became fascinated by the transformation of the mountain, and by its sculptor, the colorful genius that was my father.

They would find him perched on a ladder on the models in his studio, out in a harness on the face of the mountain, clambering here and there to get just the right perspective, or otherwise engrossed in the many details that required his constant attention. He was never too busy, however, to stop his work and explain to his visitors, whether a farmer from South Dakota or an important legislator from Washington, the meaning of the memorial and the complexities of the carving.

People from many states watched in awe as the faces of great presidents began to emerge from the massive stone cliff. One of the most famous—and enthusiastic—of these visitors was Frank Lloyd Wright, who wrote of his experience at Rushmore: "The noble countenance emerges from Rushmore as though the spirit of the mountain had heard a human prayer and itself became a human countenance."

The Work Scene

My father trained his men (who called him "the Chief") to have the most exacting standards. They were hardy men from the area, most of them down-on-their-luck miners, lumbermen, and ranchers—all proud to be part of the colossal undertaking. The pay was low, the hours long, the work hard, and the periods of employment uncertain. But morale was usually very good, and they counted themselves fortunate to have even part-time work in those hard years. Many were of a special caliber, men who had caught a glimpse of the significance of their roles in the carving of this monument that was to last throughout ages, perhaps outliving governments and nations.

Among the few skilled carvers who worked on the project were three who had studied under my father in the East—Luigi del Bianco, William S. Tallman, and Hugo Villa—and Joseph Bruner, an

These photos, taken from similar perspectives, years apart, offer a unique comparison of the monument at different stages: (1) The rear of the Washington head and the stairway and scaffolding where Jefferson would later go. (2) The finished Jefferson head, set further back into the mountain. (3) The scene today, with portions of the Roosevelt and Lincoln heads just visible in the foreground.

Foreman William Tallman seems to hang precariously *from the lower rim of the roughed-out left eye of Jefferson—actually, a scaffold within reach of his feet. (Early hand-tinted glass plate.)*

Workmen in bosun chairs drill "points" in the rough face *of Washington, while Borglum watches from below. Of the dangers in working at such heights, the sculptor said: "We needed and were developing in ourselves much courage, for much as we whistled over our job, we…were constantly aware of the proximity of… a very real graveyard all about us. Were we afraid? Certainly, we were…but I believe we enjoyed even that…became used to our situation between heaven and death and we lost thought of the hazard.*

experienced stonecutter from Indiana. Artists like these were hard to find. A number of art students were employed in the later periods of the work, as Dad liked to encourage serious students whenever he could. The students were used in the pointing and in making the constant changes necessary in the models.

The organization on the mountaintop consisted of one or two pointers, foreman, one or two powdermen, repairman, steel carrier, two to four winchmen, callboy, and as many drillers as funds and conditions would permit. Because of the erratic fund-

ing, we sometimes had only one to four men working at a time and sometimes as many as seventy, but the general average was about thirty.

The men started work at 7:30 a.m., commuting each day from surrounding towns over rough mountain trails. Before they could begin work, however, they had to climb the tortuous stairway of 760 steps which had replaced the first means of ascent to the mountaintop—a crude "chicken" ladder made of pine trees stripped of their branches, laid in crevices up the mountainside, and secured by cleats nailed to them. A small winch had been dismantled

LINCOLN BORGLUM

Five-foot plaster reproductions saved considerable time and effort and were used for comparison with the actual carving. Borglum didn't believe in "finishing" his models, preferring to prefect details in the final sculpture.

The actual carving was done with dynamite. A practical necessity.

and carried by hand up this ladder to the top, where it was reassembled to pull up the heavy cable for the tramway to the mountaintop from across the valley.

This cableway was anchored on top of the mountain on what is now the Roosevelt head, and at the bottom just south and west of the present sculptor's studio building. A steel bucket was attached to this endless cable, and a pulley placed over the load cable to carry the weight of the bucket. Supplies, which often arrived by horsedrawn wagon, were hoisted to the top by means of this cableway (including dynamite, drill steel, and the building materials for shelters for the workmen). It was not considered reliable enough to transport the men, but my father, disregarding his own safety, often rode up and down in the iron-ore bucket.

Water had to be hauled by wagon, until a better system was provided, and drinking water was hoisted to the top. An 1,800-foot, 3-inch pipeline followed the stairway, more or less, and it supplied air for the jackhammers from the compressors below. In winter weather, a liquid gas was injected in a fine mist into the pipeline beyond the compressors to prevent freezing.

Progress in Work and Equipment

As we progressed, our equipment was updated. The pipeline was enlarged and the stairway improved. It was eight years before a cable car strong enough to carry the workmen to the top was installed. This greatly increased efficiency, since it could carry three at a time—later four or five—and the men no longer need climb the exhausting stairway to the top. (They did, however, continue to walk down when work ended for the day.)

The men on the job, instead of going to work using familiar tools in a normal manner, then had to be strapped into safety harnesses and suspended over the face of the cliff, far above the rocky chasm. They worked in hot sun, merciless wind, and the bone-chilling cold fronts that brought with them temperatures of 25-30 degrees below zero, making the granite feel like ice. On only four or five days of the winter did weather keep the men from their jobs. It took a special kind of man indeed to take this kind of work!

On the mountaintop was a small village. There were buildings for the six winches for each of the heads; a repair shop with a repairman to take care of the day-to-day maintenance, also housing a supply of jackhammer parts; sheds to shelter the workmen from sudden storms and to house tools, dynamite, and caps; and a small office and studio which housed the five-foot plaster reproductions of the master models in the ground-level studio 500 feet below.

These buildings have since been removed, but a few winches remain to serve in the inspection and maintenance of the figures today.

Located at the base of the mountain was a building for the blacksmith shop, with forge, furnace, and automatic drill sharpener. All the drill steel for the jackhammers was sharpened here by the blacksmith and his helper and carried to the top via the cable. This steel would drill about a foot and a half, on an average, before it would have to be sent down for resharpening, which involved a process of heating, sharpening, reheating, and tempering before it could be sent back up. Drills were dulled and resharpened on an average of about 400 a day when work was going at full capacity.

A bunkhouse was also present in this area, and some of the men lived here. A housekeeper was provided for them; she also cooked the hot noon meals that were carried to the top by cable. The basic building complex at the base of the mountain consisted of the log studio, compressor building, blacksmith shop, bunkhouse, and a house for the operator of the cable car.

The diesel generating plant that provided power was located in Keystone, which then had a railroad for the principal purpose of carrying ore from the mines to Hill City and on to Rapid City, then east to smelters and refineries. Diesel fuel could be obtained easily by tank car, and a powerline was built to the base of Mount Rushmore to run the machinery for the actual carving. A few years after it was built our power plant mysteriously blew up. In the face of its destruction we had to buy the surplus power of a new plant built by one of the mines.

CHARLES D' EMERY

Borglum first planned to place the Jefferson *head to Washington's right (visitors at the Washington dedication may have seen this roughlikeness), but the stone developed badly here and the sculptor did not like the perspective from the road. He had it blasted from the mountain and relocated to Washington's left. This was the first and most drastic change in the design. (Early hand-tinted glass plate.)*

WORKMEN IN SWINGS

Visitors who had arrived expecting to see men carving sixty-foot heads with hammer and chisel were amazed to see such an array of tools and equipment, in an operation that bore somewhat the earmarks of a large, active quarry!

In the early stages of the work the men hung down over the side of the mountain, several hundred feet above solid ground, in what we called "bosun chairs." These were a type of swing or harness my father developed at Stone Mountain, made of heavy leather (similar to the harness tugs for horse-drawn vehicles), attached to a leather-covered seat. With a man in the seat, the tugs were passed parallel to the trunk of his body, through a spreader bar to a large ring which was in turn fastened to the cable. Above the seat a wide belt encircled the waist and was attached to a strap that passed between the wearer's legs.

Fastened into this chair, it was impossible for the occupant to fall out, even if he should lose consciousness. The chair was suspended by a 300-foot, 3/8-inch steel cable. The men—with their jackhammers and other equipment—were raised and lowered by means of the cables and the winches bolted to the mountaintop and operated by winchmen in the building there. The cables had a working load of 4,000 pounds and a breaking test of 8,000 pounds.

The winchmen on the top were not in a position to see the workmen in their swings. To relay instructions, a "callboy" was stationed so that he had a strategic view of the winchmen above and the workers in their harnesses below. As the noise level increased, we had to use microphones for the callboy to relay messages from the workmen as they wished to be moved over the face of the carving, to

The sculptor supervises the drilling, which will remove excess stone from Jefferson's left eye. Note Jackhammers on chains attached to scaffolding as safety precaution. (Early hand-tinted glass plate.)

the "steelman" (whose duty it also was to swing tools to the workmen as needed), and then to the winchmen, who heard their instructions over loudspeakers.

Each harness bore a number, to increase the ease of transmitting instructions, which might simply be "6 down" or "3 hold." Thus the workmen were free to move about over the vertical surface of the monument almost at will.

Carving With Dynamite

In the actual carving, the removal of the overburden was the first procedure. This was done with dynamite, a practical necessity in removing such a large amount of stone. (About 500,000 tons, an estimated 90 percent of the excess stone, were ultimately removed in this manner.) The use of dynamite had been suggested by a Belgian engineer to my father at the time he was experimenting with methods of stone removal at Stone Mountain. There, with the aid of a powderman from Du Pont, he perfected the method and consequently was well prepared for the challenge of Rushmore.

He had learned, in carving with dynamite, "two considerations to be borne constantly in mind—split off just what you want to remove and

Three of the faces are well developed. Teddy Rossevelt's image is just starting to appear in the 1937 historic photo. Borglum carved out each face one at a time. Since this was a new art form of historic proportions, he had to see the heads develop individually.

no more, and second, under no conditions so charge your load as to injure the stone left in place."

The process proved to be more complicated and time-consuming than it appeared in the beginning, however, and it required constant supervision. The long-exposed surface rock was badly fractured and too soft for carving, and it had to be blasted away to varying depths to reach granite solid enough for sculpturing. (Washington's chin is back 20 feet from the original surface, and Roosevelt's head is back 75 feet.) My father opted to proceed at a cautious, albeit slow rate, although blasts of 100 tons at a time were not uncommon in the early stages.

The mountain, ancient and weathered, had four deep fissures cutting through it about 70 feet apart at angles of nearly 45 degrees, sloping downward from left to right as one views the mountain.

There was no way of telling just what direction the lines of cleavage would take inside the surface until we had actually cut into the mountain and determined the stone visually. We could not avoid these fissures altogether, but we could "move" (relocate on the models) the faces forward or backward and up or down as the stone developed, to avoid the possibility that the weight of the exposed carving might cause a nose or a chin to fall off in a few hundred or a few thousand years.

CONDITION OF THE ROCK CHANGES DESIGN

So the carving involved much more than, as might be assumed, the working out of the design in the studio below and then reproducing that design on the cliff in greater dimensions. Actually, the condition of the rock forced my father to change his design a total of nine times during the work in order to fit it into the existing stone and still maintain unity of design.

In a very real way the old mountain dictated the placement and attitudes of the heads, and indeed it provided a few surprises of its own. For instance, the particularly large feldspar crystals in Washington's lapel, and the silver and lead at the end of Lincoln's nose. Also, the curious, reddish mineral (allanite) that necessitated the turning of the Jefferson head in order to bring it into the hollow between cheek and nose where it could be removed.

To accomplish the dynamiting, the workmen were lowered to their assigned places to drill parallel holes in the surface of the mountain. At first the holes were deep (6 to 8 feet) and closely spaced (15 to 18 inches) in a string of 15 to 20 placed 2 to 3 feet in front of the next row. Powder magazines were located in crevices in the stone and as the drilling of each row was completed the "powder monkey" would come along and place several sticks of powder in them, tamping the rest of the space with

August 30, 1936: Franklin D. Roosevelt, on a tour of drought-stricken states, is on hand to help dedicate the Jefferson head, along with South Dakota's Senator Bulow and Governor Berry. Sculptor Borglum demonstrates to the president the intricacies of mountain carving. F.D.R. called the sculpture a "monument and inspiration to democratic government not only in our own country but throughout the world."

LINCOLN BORGLUM COLLECTION

damp sand to absorb the jarring effect of the blast and thus protect the remaining stone. The driller would then move up and behind the row of holes and repeat the process. (Drillers were always moved in the "up" direction so that if by some chance the line of holes was accidentally set off he would be above the charge and out of danger.)

Our practice was to "blow off" the morning's work at noon, when we were on top for lunch, and at four in the afternoon, when work had ended for the day. So twice daily great blasts echoed throughout the surrounding canyons as tons of granite crashed down the mountainside. In this way the scarred and fissured outer rock was removed, leaving a surface of solid rock ready for the actual carving.

As the work progressed and we came closer to the surface we wanted to protect, holes were drilled closer together and not so deep, and the explosive charge was reduced. In the final blasting many of the holes contained no dynamite at all, and only a blasting cap was used as a charge, removing the rock with amazing accuracy. In fact, the drillers became so skilled in their ability to remove the right amount of stone in the right location without damaging the rest of the carving, that they could block out a nose to within an inch of the finished surface, shape the lips, and grade the contours of the neck, cheeks, and brows.

Precision Work and the Artist's Touch

When we came to the precision work to be done without blasting, scaffolding of heavy bridge timber was constructed in eight-foot stories and bolted to six-inch projections that had been left on the granite surface for this purpose and reinforced with steel. Dad had spent much of his life on scaffolds and took great care in providing his men with a safe, solid, comfortable platform from which to work. The scaffolds enabled us to work year-round, since we could cover them with canvas as protection against the raw winter weather and even heat them with wood-burning heaters made from oil drums.

The final six or so inches of granite were taken off with pneumatic tools, mostly drilling down from the top, with holes as close together as possible, and the web between was cut out with another type of pneumatic tool, a "channel iron." The excess stone was then broken off with wedges and hand hammers, after which the surface was again honeycombed with drills in a series of horizontal, parallel holes, and the stone between was removed with hand chisels.

Although we were able to transfer the measurements to the mountain to a tolerance of a quarter-inch, there was no way mechanically to correct for perspective. This had to be done by the eye of the artist. The three inches of stone left over the surface allowed the margin my father needed to work with and make his corrections, the artist's touch that would give life and vitality to the sculpture.

My father examined the progress in various lights at different angles and distances, from dawn to dusk, working out the smallest detail by studying light and shadow, almost exactly as he would have done in his studio, except that it took much longer. In a January 11, 1947, article in the Saturday Evening Post, William J. Bulow, who had served as governor of South Dakota and United States Senator, reflected on my father's ability:

...No other man has ever had the perspective to carve such gigantic figures and make them look natural to the human eye from any spot below. Several times I climbed into the basket and rode up the cable to the mountaintop and inspected the carvings.... The closeup view is disappointing.

You cannot see the face of Lincoln when you stand on his lower eyelid; you cannot see Washington while walking back and forth on his lower lip. It takes a genius to figure out the proper perspective so that the carvings will look right from the point from which the human eye beholds them. Gutzon Borglum was that genius.

On one occasion I was visiting him at his studio at the foot of the mountain. We were out on the porch looking up at the mountaintop, where a number of men were working on the carvings. He said Washington wasn't right. His head did not sit right. He was going to turn the head around a little. I asked him how in Sam Hill he was going to turn Washington's head around in the solid granite of the mountain. He took me into his studio and showed me his model, pointing out how he would chisel off a little here and a little there. I could not see his point at all. But a few months after that, I was up there again, and Gutzon Borglum had turned the head of Washington around. — WILLIAM J. BULOW

FROM SCAFFOLDS TO CAGES

In the final phase of the work, scaffolds were removed and the men took to working over the final surface from the cables. This time, however, the cables were fastened to wooden "cages," either three by four feet suspended from one cable, or three by eight feet suspended from two cables, depending on whether one or two men were to work in the cage. These cages, transferred from one position to another by means of the winches on top, gave us the power of mobility we needed and still gave the men a firm platform from which to work.

From an artist's standpoint, the cage had another advantage. It could be located in an eye or a nostril and when the men inside had removed the stone as instructed after careful study from below, the cage could be pulled away from the mountain to further study the effect from various viewpoints. Again, this final finishing was carried out much as it would have been in a studio, except for the mechanics and time involved in correcting a feature. In the studio a nostril could be changed in a few minutes by reshaping the soft clay; on the mountain the same work might take several days and many trips to the mountaintop and back to study the effects.

The final surface was obtained with a pneumatic "bumper," similar to a jackhammer, that bounced over the surface, leaving a texture comparable to a cement sidewalk. Most of the final design was made with this tool, emphasizing or softening features of the figures as the design required.

So the work was generally done in three stages: In the first the men accomplished the heavy blasting, hanging over the mountain in bosun chairs; second came the work from the scaffolding; and finally the finishing work from the hanging cages. It was not quite that simple, however, since all three of these phases were often going on at the same time on different parts of the carving.

In each stage the normal sequence of work was measuring, drilling, blasting, drilling, wedging, and bumping. All four heads were blocked out and their positions on the design determined before finishing details on any were begun.

LINCOLN BORGLUM

***J**uly 2, 1939: Theodore Roosevelt, with his famous squint, peers at the crowd as the flag is pulled away in the final of six colorful dedications. Roosevelt had said, "If a monument is ever built to me, I hope Gutzon Borglum does it." (This is one of several historic construction photos in this book taken by Lincoln Borglum, whose work made the covers of such magazines as "Liberty," "Collier's," and "The Saturday Evening Post.")*

A Safety Record to be Proud Of

We were proud of our safety record on the mountain. In spite of the great and ever-present hazards, our precautions were such that, in all the 14 years the work covered, not one man was killed or even seriously injured on the job. The men always worked in staggered positions so that dropped equipment wouldn't fall on another below. Masks were furnished to protect them from inhaling the granite dust which might result in silicosis, a disease all Black Hills miners dread.

Only two accidents, both minor ones, occurred in all this time. One was caused by a caprice of nature. We heard distant thunder but ignored it—summer storms here were common and the sun was still shining on Mount Rushmore. But suddenly a lightning bolt from out of the blue exploded the dynamite being prepared by a driller for the next detonation, flinging him out into space on his cable. Fortunately his reflexes took over, and by bending his knees and using his feet to kick the granite as he swung back to the surface of the mountain, he was able to keep from smashing into it. His injuries were only slight, but from that day on, no one worked with dynamite if a thunderstorm was brewing anywhere around. (This same thunderbolt blew the shoes from a young man who was guiding a group of sightseers up the mountain at the time.)

The second mishap was caused by an equipment failure. Five workmen riding in the tramway were nearing the top when a shearpin in the cable pulley broke. As the car hurtled to the bottom, all five landed on the handle of the emergency brake, snapping it instantly. Foreman Matty Rielly quickly grabbed a two-by-four and stuck it between the cable and wheel of the hoist, slowing the runaway's descent. Only one man was injured, again only slightly, when he impulsively jumped to the ground as the car neared bottom. There weren't many things that could shake the nerves of these stalwart men!

Unveiling Ceremonies and Dedications

People continued to flock to the mountain in ever-increasing numbers. By 1936 the Jefferson head was ready to be unveiled, and on August 30 great blasts were set off, the flag pulled away to reveal the huge face, and another flag hoisted. A cheering crowd of 3,000 heard President Franklin D. Roosevelt deliver an impromptu speech in which he admitted that until that moment he had not fully realized the "permanent importance" of the monument.

This ceremony was followed on September 17, 1937, by the dedication of the Lincoln head, the date chosen as the 150th anniversary of the adoption of the Constitution. The crowd, this time 5,000 people, came to hear an address by Nebraska Senator Edward R. Burke and another by the sculptor, who never failed to give the people the splendid oratory they had come to expect from him. After the speeches the flag swung away to reveal the bearded, solemn face of Lincoln. (My father, after much study and thought, had decided to carve a bearded Lincoln, instead of a beardless Lincoln like the one in the Capitol. He felt it would show more strength and would be more familiar to the people.)

About 12,000 people gathered for the unveiling of Teddy Roosevelt's head (modeled after a bust my father had done in 1918). This was July 2, 1939, nine years after the dedication of Washington, the first figure. It was also the occasion of the 50th anniversary of South Dakota's statehood, so nothing was withheld in making this a memorable celebration. It was an evening performance, lighted first by a brilliant moon, then by dramatic fireworks, and finally by huge searchlights. William S. Hart of silent-movie fame was there, as were Sioux Indians in full native regalia, and other notables.

A final dedication was planned for 1941, but in the face of my father's death and the imminence of war it was postponed several times and then forgotten altogether. Thus no dedication on a par with the importance of the monument was ever held for Mount Rushmore. (On July 3, 1991, more than five years after Lincoln Borglum's death, President George Bush presided at a formal dedication of the memorial combined with the celebration of Mount Rushmore's 50th year.)

A Record for the Future

The first plan for the memorial, as dedicated by President Coolidge in 1927, called for an entablature, or inscription, to be carved on the face of the mountain, a history of about 500 words to describe the eight crucial events in the history of the United States from 1776 to 1904 (from Washington to Roosevelt). This was to be about 80 by 120 feet in the shape of the Louisiana Purchase, and placed in about the location of the present Lincoln head.

It was originally planned that Coolidge would write the text for this history, but arguments ensued when it was found my father had "edited" Coolidge's first submission. (Most felt this was his prerogative as the final arbiter of anything that was to go on the mountain.) The whole episode was aggravated all out of proportion by the gleeful newspaper accounts of the day, and as a result Coolidge became miffed and never finished the writing.

This aerial view locates the site of Borglum's Hall of Records in the canyon behind the heads. Borglum's dream for leaving a record explaining the importance of the memorial to future generations was realized in 1998 with the completion of a vault at the original location. A granite capstone covers 16 porcelain enamel panels within a sealed case explaining how and why the memorial was carved.

The plan was given up anyway, but for two, more critical reasons. After considerable experimenting with painting some of the lettering on the mountainside, it was found that if they were to be legible from any distance the letters must be so large that there would not be room for 500 words, and they would have to be cut so deeply (to last as long as the heads) that the whole idea became impractical.

The second reason was that it had been found that this section of the mountain would be needed for the Lincoln head, as a result of the relocation of Jefferson. (Later the history idea was revived in a national contest sponsored by the Hearst newspapers and judged by a 14-member committee of judges that included Franklin D. and Eleanor Roosevelt. The college edition winning entry by William Andrew Burkett appears in bronze in the Borglum Memorial View Terrace.)

In the face of the technical difficulties encountered in this plan, another, more lasting plan was developed. Directly behind the four heads, separating them from the rest of the mountain, a canyon about the depth of the Lincoln head runs from the right of Lincoln to the left of Washington, as viewed from the ground. On the wall of the canyon, directly opposite the back of the Roosevelt head, a room about 80 feet long and 60 feet wide would be cut into the solid wall of the mountain.

On the walls of this room would be carved a brief history of the United States in three languages. Aluminum plates containing important historical documents, including the Constitution and the Declaration of Independence...busts of famous personages...and a list of U.S. contributions to the world in science, industry, and the arts would be sealed in the walls. It was to be called the "Hall of Records" and would be reached by a stone and concrete stairway.

Lack of time and funds eventually halted work on the hall, for which the entrance—a drift cut into the mountain about 80 feet—had been blocked out. As originally planned, 100 feet of solid stone would have been left above the hall, making the inscriptions inside much less vulnerable to the ravages of time than the exposed heads themselves.

My father was convinced that the hall was necessary to complete the memorial. As he put it, the hall would be like a "caption," or "signature." It would tell of the civilization that produced and molded the presidents whose faces were carved into the mountain and tell the history of the nation to that date.

To him it was unthinkable that any monument, especially one that would last well over 100,000 years, should not have a label and inscription, or at least an explanation. He often referred to such perplexing mysteries as the Easter Island heads and said that as an advanced civilization we owed it to future generations to leave definitive records.

At one time a bill providing for the hall did pass Congress, but an appropriation for it was never made. My father's carefully detailed plans are still in existence, and with our modern technology and affluence the hall could still be completed. I, too, believe we should not leave an enigma for future generations.

RIKKI THOMPSON

*Indeed I wonder
if in my father's critical
eyes it would ever
have been finished.*

A Monument for the Ages

As it turned out, the course of my own life was also more or less dictated by the mountain. By 1931, when work on the mountain had been in progress for less than four years, I was nineteen, having completed high school, two years of prep school, and a year of private employment, all the while spending my summers helping my father in South Dakota.

That particular summer our family had just returned from Europe, where my father had unveiled, in Poznan, Poland, his statue of Woodrow Wilson (later destroyed by Hitler's troops), made for his friend Paderewski. I was preparing to enter the University of Virginia to study engineering. Upon our return my father fired one of his key men (for cutting too deeply) and needed a replacement. By that time Major Tucker had gone and Dad was already spending more time in South Dakota than planned. He asked me to help him out "for a while," and I reluctantly agreed. I'd had my heart set on college, but still the enormity of the work fascinated me, and I felt Dad really needed me. My first job was that of pointer, and I keenly felt its importance and responsibility.

We worked late into the fall—too late for me to go to school—so when the work started up again in the spring I was back on the job. Again fall came, the mountain made its demands, and again school was postponed. By that time I was completely caught up in the work and its message, so finally, in 1934, I gave up my plans for college altogether. Besides, af-

From some viewpoints only certain faces appear. And yet the position and form is complete. This aerial view presents a unique view of the finished faces and the untouched granite domes of the Harney Range.

This aerial view is a dramatic sweep *of the overall construction scene as it appeared just prior to the memorial's completion.*

ter two years of no pay (my father could be a most persuasive man), I had made the payroll at last—55 cents an hour! A compelling reason for a young man getting started in the cattle business.

From then on I worked on the mountain until the work stopped for good in 1941, participating in every facet of the construction from the placing of explosive charges to operating the jackhammers. I was to have complete knowledge of all the work and the capability to carry on any phase, should some key man need to be replaced.

I progressed to foreman, then superintendent of all construction work in 1938. The latter position involved responsibility for the placement of the men, the carving, pointing, purchasing of materials, and supervising the WPA program that was going on at the base of the mountain. (At Rushmore, federal WPA money was used to improve parking areas, walkways, and the water system and restrooms for an ever-increasing number of visitors.)

My father always retained the master's hand, but now left more and more of the details of opera-

tion to me, confidently leaving notes such as this for me and my pointing crew to carry out:

I want you, in beginning the work and allotting the positions to the men, to avoid the two finished faces completely. Do not touch the hairlines around the face of Washington or his chin, or under his chin. Do not approach the face lines of Jefferson, or to the side of his face or under his chin.

On photograph No. 1, I have drawn a circle where you can locate Payne to begin down-drilling under what will be Washington's ear and the left-hand lapel of his coat. Put one or two men on the lapel, which I have marked No. 2. Put two men on Washington's shoulders and work carefully from the top, which I have marked No. 3. That will dispose of five or six men.

I have marked Lincoln's eye. You can put two men in cages in each of the eyes. I would use Ander-

son on the one side and Bianco on the other, putting Bianco where the feldspar streaks run down, and Anderson on the outside. I would give Payne, with Bianco, a position on the nose and have them begin to take off stone by drilling in squares and breaking it off down to within six or seven inches of the finished surface. But do not try to cut the eyelid or eyeball. Make a round mass for each of these. Lincoln's face in that way will take up probably six more men.

You can put about three men on the Roosevelt stone, marking carefully the contour of Lincoln's face so that none of that is disturbed, and going back into the hole next to Jefferson's face as deep as you can. If you can put any men down on the block that I have marked No. 8, without any danger of tools and stone falling on them, all right. I would put about three men on the big crag. We still have seventy or eighty feet to take off that. I think this will keep you busy until I get there.

Still later, after my father's death, I became the sculptor in charge of the commission. Then, when the memorial was completed, was appointed its first superintendent under the National Park Service, serving in that capacity until 1944. So my father's mountain came to dominate my life, perhaps as much as his own.

NOT A PROFITABLE VENTURE

Wages had never been high on the mountain (in 1933 unskilled workers were making 50 cents an hour, drillers 65 cents, and skilled carvers $1). I spent my spare time developing my cattle business at the family ranch near Hermosa. Dad accepted other commissions, and mother was kept busy promoting the mountain, trying to straighten out my father's finances (so sorely strained by Rushmore), and entertaining all the people—from famous personages to art students—who constantly found their way to Rushmore.

My father's commission had never been adjusted to include the extra work he assumed when Tucker left, and he often bought materials himself or turned back money paid him by the commission, enabling him to keep the work going a little longer.

Many of the commissions he earned during this time were likewise loaned to the work. All in all the memorial was not a profitable venture for its sculptor, or for the Borglum family—the total paid him for the 16 years he was involved with the mountain was about $170,000.

Fame, however, is compensation of a kind, and the mountain did assure my father his place in history, regardless of how his other works might be assessed in the future. For Rushmore captured the imagination not of an individual, a city, state, or region, but of an entire nation and that was the result he had worked for. Today, he would feel repaid many times over if he could see the throngs who come to view the memorial each day. He never valued money highly anyway; he thought it should not even be a prime consideration when a great idea was under discussion.

HUSBAND, FATHER, AND SCULPTOR

Dad was nearing 60 when the work on the mountain began, but he was a vigorous and energetic man, and he adapted to the rugged demands of the mountain better than many men much younger. But the years inevitably began to tell on him, and his old fire and drive gradually diminished. Even so, he never failed to respond to any opportunity to stump for his mountain, and an invitation to go on a speaking tour of the Midwest early in 1941 was willingly accepted.

I drove Mother and Dad to the station in Rapid City, where they took the train. (My mother often accompanied him on such trips, for they always enjoyed being together.) The railroad parallels the highway to Hermosa for a way, and as I was driving back to the ranch by myself, I followed it until the tracks and the highway diverged, and I had the strangest feeling that I was never going to see my father again.

He died suddenly in Chicago on March 6, 1941, the result of a minor operation. He was 74. My mother was with him, and my sister, Mary Ellis Vhay, and I arrived shortly before he died, but he was already unconscious. We mourned him, not as the brilliant, flamboyant sculptor the world knew, but as a man who had been husband and father to us in the fullest sense—perhaps not always wise, but always gentle, always loving. We were consoled by the knowledge that he had lived a life rich in activity and fulfillment. For him there had been no missed opportunities, no sorrowful regrets.

He had lived to see a large part of his most ambitious undertaking take shape, though it was by no means finished. (Indeed I wonder if in my father's

Borglum was a master of detail. Roosevelt's spectacles are partially illusion, skillfully created to complete his familiar countenance. His mustache and Lincoln's beard were purposely left with a rough texture.

critical eyes it would ever have been finished.) Now, as sculptor in charge of the commission, I determined with the help of the loyal crew to complete the monument—insofar as funds would permit.

THE FUNDING ENDS—THE CARVING STOPS

Anyone who has studied the original model and other early models (now at the Borglum Ranch and Studio) will realize that the figures were to have been finished to the waists, including such details as period clothing and hands, which at the time of my father's death had not even been started. Even parts of some of the faces and hairstyles were incomplete. (The hair had been left until last so that the tops of the heads could be used as a base of operations.) Very little of the Hall of Records, which my father considered vital, had been roughed out. Then there was the immense pile of rubble from the blastings, which my father had planned to remove. But only a small amount of money remained.

Times were tense in 1941. Europe was at war, and there were rumors that America would soon be involved. Realizing that no more money would be

forthcoming, I decided to use the remaining funds on the refining of the four faces, carrying out the techniques my father had originated for bringing as lifelike a look as possible to each face. As we finished the heads, eight months after my father's death, I thought of all I would have liked to accomplish and wished that events had allowed me the opportunity.

On October 31, 1941, the last drilling was done on Mount Rushmore and all the fissures sealed with a mixture of granite dust and white lead. We removed all of the machinery and most of the buildings from the top of the mountain, took down the cable car, and stored all this material in buildings at the foot of the mountain. (These buildings have now all been removed, as was the first studio, then located on the site of the present Borglum Viewing Terrace.)

By this time, considerable improvements had been made in the Doane Mountain installations (from which the public now views the monument), and on highways, parking areas, and the enlarged memorial surroundings in general. We were still liv-

Construction on the "Hall of Records" was halted in 1939 after merely carving the entrance. (Early Kodacrome, 1935.)

– 43 –

*R*ushmore as Borglum saw it in 1925 — *A*nd the way visitors see it today.

ing at the ranch. Impetuous and generous to a fault, my father had not been the wisest in managing his personal finances, and it was three years before my mother and I finally paid the last of his debts.

In the beginning it was estimated that the memorial would cost about $400,000 and take about four years to complete. Although some felt my father had grossly underestimated the cost, there was no real way of knowing what it would cost and how long it would take since there was no comparable work on which to base estimates. We certainly did not dream it would take 14 years to complete and that the actual cost would be close to $1 million ($989,992.32, to be exact).

The major cause for the delay was the erratic funding. We were shut down for a total of 7.5 of those 14 years—sometimes for two or three months at a time, sometimes six months or longer. South Dakota and the nation were hard hit by drought and depression. It was easier to get funds for WPA workers to build steps, walls, and walks than it was to get money to continue the carving. Had the work progressed in a more orderly manner, I feel sure it could have been done in five years and at about the original estimate.

The major item in the memorial's cost was in the removal of stone. Figured on this basis alone, not including the many other operations involved in the work, the cost was less than $2 per ton for the 500,000 tons of granite removed. Not much, especially considering that in the process the granite left on the mountain was in the form of a masterpiece that would last for the ages, an example of the precision of the sculptor's art on a scale never attempted before in all of history.

In the final analysis the federal government paid $836,000 of the total cost. Actually Mount Rushmore turned out to be one of its soundest financial investments. Aside from taxes on increased income to South Dakotans, the federal tax alone on the gas used by those who come to visit the memorial amounts to many millions of dollars each year. From 1941 to the present time, over 100 million people have traveled here to view the memorial.

Mount Rushmore Universally Accepted

The state of South Dakota, too, has profited hugely—just as Doane Robinson, Senator Norbeck, Congressmen Williamson and Case, and the many others who so staunchly stood behind the project for so many years had envisioned. South Dakota's legislature never did come through with an appropriation for the monument (much to the embarrassment of Robinson), but it did spend huge amounts on highways and in advertising the once remote and lonely mountain. The memorial has changed the economy of the state. Tourism has brought literally hundreds of millions of dollars into the state, to make this industry second only to agriculture in revenue.

Mount Rushmore has become universally accepted as one of the world's great monuments. Aside from the matter of craftsmanship, which most experts agree is excellent, in size alone the monument stands unsurpassed. The stone removed from the memorial during the course of the work was approximately twice the volume used to construct the Great Sphinx at Giza. The entire head of the Sphinx (from chin to the top of its head) is not quite as long as Washington's nose! (It has been stated that 100,000 men worked 20 years to construct the Egyptian sculpture.)

Borglum in 1934, at age 67. (Early hand-tinted glass plate.)

John Gutzon de la Mothe Borglum always had a broad view of life. Born in 1867 in a log cabin on America's western frontier (near Bear Lake, Idaho), he spent his boyhood on the wide prairies of Nebraska, the oldest in the large household of his doctor father, a Danish immigrant. Early in life his horizons began to expand when at 17 he left home to go to California to study painting, at which he excelled, and later to England, France, and Spain, where his skill and reputation grew. But gradually he turned from his brushes to the chisel, finally devoting himself exclusively to sculpture, an art form he loved. His works brought him high honors and eventually made him a world-famous figure—even before he began his masterpiece at Rushmore.

But art did not consume all the Borglum energies. He was an eloquent and prolific writer, an engineer and inventor, an orator with a gift for politics (useful in raising funds for the memorial). He worked with the Army Corps of Engineers to design the light for the Statue of Liberty, and played an important role in World War I by investigating and exposing dangerous shortcomings in the manufacture of American aircraft. He was active in civic beautification, in parks and conservation, and originated detailed plans far ahead of his time for a huge network of federal highways. There were Borglum plans for flood control, Borglum plans for energy.

Quick to espouse any cause in which he believed, and with an opinion on every subject, he was an oft-quoted and sometimes controversial figure. (When he heard that the Oglala Sioux were starving in the drought and depression of the thirties at their Pine Ridge, South Dakota, reservation, Borglum—not waiting for responses to his many letters to politicians—rounded up cattle and clothing for the stricken tribe.) His personal magnetism was tremendous, and he numbered among his friends many of the famous artists, statesmen, leaders of industry, philosophers, planners, and presidents of his time.

But Borglum—large as his world had become—never lost touch with the people of America. And it was his special feeling for them, together with his passionate devotion to American ideals, that inspired the concept behind the memorial and gave it artistic expression on a scale so grand that Rushmore truly stands alone among the great monuments of the world.

In his talk "Why the Mountain Memorial?" for the Collier's Radio Hour, January 18, 1931, 8:40 p.m., my father brought the matter of the sculpture's colossal proportions vividly home to his listening audience:

The faces of Washington, Jefferson, Lincoln, and Roosevelt on Mount Rushmore are sixty feet; the figures [if] finished [completely] would be 450 feet. If they stood in the falls of Niagara they would block the great cataract. If they should sit in the falls, this mighty river would only splash about their ears. If they should walk down the East River to the Hudson, they could barely creep under the great bridges. They would swamp most of the smaller vessels, and when they reached the Statue of Liberty, they would have to stoop to read by her dimming light.

Mount Rushmore—truly a monument for the ages!

All About Mount Rushmore National Monument

Mount Rushmore History Association

The mission of the nonprofit Mount Rushmore History Association is to support and assist the National Park Service with educational, historical and interpretive activities at Mount Rushmore National Memorial. The Association has contributed over $715,000 to the Memorial since its founding in 1993.

It funds special events throughout the year, contributes to educational programs, provides free publications for visitors, and supplies the flags for the Avenue of Flags. Please call 1-800-699-3142 for more information.

Mount Rushmore Contact Information

By Mail
13000 Highway 244
Building 31, Suite1
Keystone, SD 57751-0268

By Phone
Headquarters
605-574-2523

**Visitor Information
Recorded Message**
605-574-3171

By Fax
605-574-2307

Granite fragment with drill holes.
Photo by Ricki Thompson

MOUNT RUSHMORE

Junior Ranger

There is a one-hour series of ranger-led activities for children during the summer months. Parents come along, too. The events start daily. Learn more about Mount Rushmore National Memorial with the free Junior Ranger Activity Book. Fun activities help you explore the park, its history, and its heritage. When the activities are done, you can get a certificate for a free Junior Ranger badge or, for a small fee, upgrade to the Junior Ranger Patch!

SUGGESTED READING

BORGLUM CARTER, ROBIN. *Gutzon Borglum: His Life and Work.* Austin, Texas: Eakin Press, 1998.

FITE, GILBERT. *Mount Rushmore.* Pierre, South Dakota: Mount Rushmore History Association, 1952.

HIGBEE, PAUL. *Mount Rushmore's Hall of Records.* Pierre, South Dakota: Mount Rushmore History Association, 1999.

SHAFF, HOWARD AND AUDREY KARL. *Six Wars at a Time.* Freeman, South Dakota: Permelia Press, 1985.

SMITH, REX ALAN. *The Carving of Mount Rushmore.* New York: Abbeville Press, 1985.

NATIONAL PARK SERVICE

National Park Service employees perform a routine inspection of each of the great heads in the huge carving each year, patching where necessary. They are strapped into harnesses and raised and lowered by winches in much the same way the workmen were moved about over the face of the carving over 50 years ago.

The hard granite of the memorial is extremely resistant to weather, but its sculptor realized that water accumulating in the cracks would expand with freezing and could eventually damage the carving. Borglum devised a compound to fill the cracks, forcing the rain and melted snow to run off without harm. All the cracks were sealed with this mixture before work on the sculpture ceased in 1941, and the Park Service used the formula for many years in annual maintenance checks. In 1990, a structural stability study of the mountain determined that Borglum's old "recipe" should be replaced, so a silicone building sealant is now used in the annual repair work.

The study also identified 144 structural gaps (cracks) and found that these formed 21 distinct rock blocks that make up the mountain. The blocks are structurally significant because they could move from their current position into a position of instability. No such instabilities currently exist, but the National Park Service installed a monitoring system in 1998 intended to track the movement of these blocks. The annual maintenance program of patching the cracks and monitoring the rock blocks will ensure long-term preservation of Mount Rushmore National Memorial.

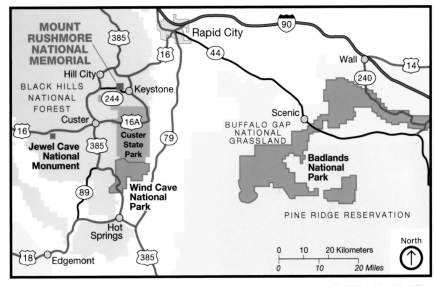

DETAIL MAP

Mount Rushmore Today

Mount Rushmore National Memorial is administered by the National Park Service, open year-round, the memorial provides interpretive programs by Park Service personnel during the summer; seminars and other special events are scheduled throughout the year.

As a national memorial Rushmore is unique. Pictures of Mount Rushmore are almost universally recognized. It is a satisfaction to know that long after the passing of its sculptor—long after generations of his descendants have come and gone--there - in the center of the continent his monument will stand, an astonishing, enduring record of the history of the United States and an eloquent testament to his love for his country.

I want, somewhere in America on or near the Rockies, the backbone of the Continent, so far removed from succeeding, selfish, coveting civilizations, a few feet of stone that bears witness, carries the likenesses, the dates, a word or two of the great things we accomplished as a Nation, placed so high it won't pay to pull down for lesser purposes.

Hence, let us place there, carved high, as close to heaven as we can, the words of our leaders, their faces, to show posterity what manner of men they were. Then breathe a prayer that these records will endure until the wind and the rain alone shall wear them away.

—GUTZON BORGLUM

*T*he warmth of sunrise suggests the warmth of the real-life Lincoln as he gazes with compassion on the great nation he preserved and inspired.

KC Publications has been the leading publisher of colorful, interpretive books about National Park areas, public lands, Indian lands, and related subjects for over 45 years. We have 5 active series—over 125 titles—with Translation Packages in up to 8 languages for over half the areas we cover. Write, call, or visit our web site for our full-color catalog.

Our series are:

The Story Behind the Scenery® – Compelling stories of over 65 National Park areas and similar Public Land areas. Some with Translation Packages.

in pictures... Nature's Continuing Story®– A companion, pictorially oriented, series on America's National Parks. All titles have Translation Packages.

For Young Adventurers® – Dedicated to young seekers and keepers of all things wild and sacred. Explore America's Heritage from A to Z.

Voyage of Discovery® – Exploration of the expansion of the western United States.

Indian Culture and the Southwest – All about Native Americans, past and present.

To receive our full-color catalog featuring over 125 titles—Books and other related specialty products:
Call (800) 626-9673, fax (928) 684-5189, write to the address below, or visit our web sites at www.kcpublications.com

Published by KC Publications, P.O. Box 3615, Wickenburg, AZ 85358

Inside back cover: *George Washington—the first choice for the memorial. Photo by K.C. DenDooven.*

Back cover: *Avenue of Flags Photo by Mary Liz Austin*

Created, Designed, and Published in the U.S.A.
Printed by Tien Wah Press (Pte.) Ltd, Singapore
Pre-Press by United Graphic Pte. Ltd